WESTERN DIAMONDBACK RATTLESNAKE

GARY SPROTT

WORLD'S COOLEST SNAKES

Rourke
Educational Media
rourkeeducationalmedia.com

Fast Facts

Family: Viperidae

Genus: Crotalus Linnaeus

Number of species: 44

Species: Crotalus atrox

Diet: Mice, rabbits, rats, chipmunks, squirrels

Range: Southwestern United States, including Arizona, California, New Mexico, Oklahoma and Texas, and northern Mexico

WORLD'S COOLEST SNAKES

Table of Contents

Rugged Rattler 4

Night Stalker 10

Snake and Shake 16

Round 'Em Up! 22

Glossary 30

Index 31

Show What You Know 31

Further Reading 31

About the Author 32

Rugged Rattler

With its famous noise-making tail and **distinctive** scales shaped like diamonds, the western diamondback rattlesnake is a popular symbol of America's Wild West.

One of the largest **species** of snakes native to the United States, the deadly western diamondback (Crotalus atrox) can grow up to 6 feet (1.8 meters) in length and live for more than 20 years.

5

The western diamondback isn't a fussy house-hunter. It can make its home in canyons, scrubland, deserts, and grasslands. It will even settle into a comfy pile of garbage or a good ol' heap of junk—anywhere it can find some yummy rats, rabbits, squirrels, or chipmunks for dinner!

An Extra-Long Ruler

The western diamondback would seem kind of **puny** next to the world's longest venomous snake. The king cobra can stretch up to 18 feet (5.5 meters). That's nearly as long as a full-size pickup truck!

◀◀ *Western diamondbacks can escape the sizzling sun in cool canyons like these.*

Western diamondbacks are **cunning** hunters. The snake coils up and waits patiently and quietly to strike in a sneak attack. But it can also give chase, even slithering up a tree or slinking through a stream to grab its next meal!

Fact or Fiction?

The western diamondback can hear noises over long distances.

FICTION! Snakes don't have ears. The rattlesnake knows when prey or predators are on the move nearby because it feels the ground vibrating.

Night Stalker

Like Goldilocks with her porridge, the western diamondback rattlesnake doesn't like things too hot or too cold. The cold-blooded reptile stays out of the summer sun as much as possible, taking shelter underground or finding a shady spot in the rocks.

Let Me Keep Sleeping, Guys!

When the temperature starts to drop, these critters head to a cozy cave or snug burrow for the winter. Hundreds of rattlesnakes may **hibernate** together in these community dens.

Fact or Fiction?

Western diamondbacks protect humans from life-threatening diseases.

FACT! By eating rats and mice, the rattlesnake helps stop the spread of dangerous viruses carried by rodents.

The western diamondback is mostly **nocturnal**, slinking out at sundown to hunt when its surroundings have cooled.

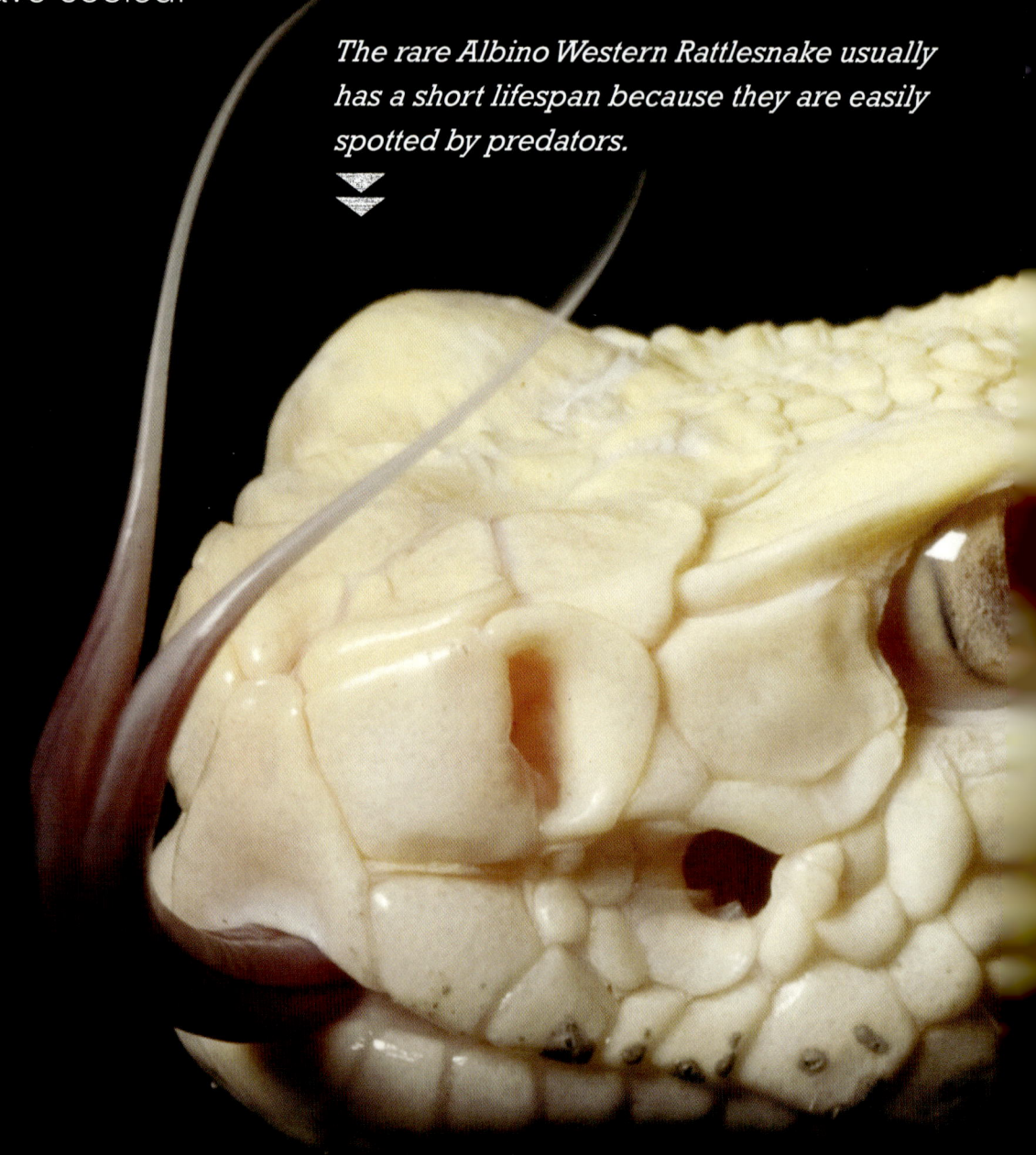

The rare Albino Western Rattlesnake usually has a short lifespan because they are easily spotted by predators.

The rattlesnake is a member of the pit viper family, a type of snake that has a small hole between each eye and nostril. The diamondback uses these tiny pits to sense heat from warm-blooded animals, allowing it to track its prey even in the dark of night.

Killer snakes like the western diamondback use their fangs to inject their prey with **venom**. The rattlesnake's curved fangs can be up to six inches (15 centimeters) long and fold flat when the snake closes its mouth—ready to flick back into action like switchblades!

After killing its prey with its fatal bite, the western diamondback swallows its meal whole—even if dinner weighs more than the chef! Burp! It's no wonder the rattler may not feel hungry again for weeks.

Snake and Shake

Do you bite your fingernails? Don't worry, we won't tell mom. Well, your nails may taste a little bit like a western diamondback's rattle. But please don't try to find out for yourself—this rattle is nothing to toy with!

The snake's shaker is a series of hollow rings at the tip of its tail. The rings are made from a **protein** called keratin—yup, the same stuff that's in your nails and hair.

The rattlesnake uses its amazing noisemaker when hunting to confuse its prey. The rattle also acts like a security alarm to shoo away possible attackers.

17

to 60 times a second! So, it's no surprise these vibrating rings can break as they get older. But there's no need for the rattlesnake to get in a tizzy—a new ring grows whenever it sheds its skin.

▲ *A western diamondback can add a new rattle two or three times a year.*

Ricky, Is That You?

The western diamondback's nickname is "coon tail." That comes from the black and white bands near the rattle, making it look like a raccoon's tail.

juvenile western diamondback

Each spring, male western diamondbacks compete in body-wrestling bouts. The champion of the ring gets to mate with a female. Baby rattlers develop in eggs inside their mother. Like kittens and puppies, rattlesnakes are born live in a **litter**.

Fact or Fiction?

After mating, the female western diamondback settles into a nest of leaves and twigs until her babies are born.

FICTION! The king cobra of Southeast Asia is the only species of snake in the world that builds a nest for its eggs.

What, No Babysitter?

Diamondbacks don't have much of a childhood. Soon after these shiny new crawlers are born, their mother slinks away for good!

Newborn diamondbacks are about 10 inches (25 centimeters) long. They don't have a rattle because they haven't shed their skin yet. But, warning: These precious little jewels come with fangs and a venom-filled bite.

Round 'Em Up!

The western diamondback rattlesnake is found across the southwestern United States and northern Mexico. Its natural predators include hawks, eagles, bobcats, coyotes, and roadrunners.

western diamondback rattlesnake

Hissssssssin' Cousins!

Dozens of rattlesnake **species** are found across the Americas. The western diamondback and its cousin, the eastern diamondback, are among the largest and the most common in North America.

eastern diamondback rattlesnake

Eastern and western diamondback rattlesnakes are to blame for about 95 percent of snakebite deaths in the United States.

CAUTION

THERE MAY BE RATTLESNAKES IN THIS AREA. RATTLESNAKES ARE ACTIVE AT NIGHT DURING THE SUMMER. THEY WILL SEEK OUT SHADY PLACES DURING THE HEAT OF THE DAY. CHILDREN SHOULD BE WARNED NOT TO GO NEAR ANY SNAKE. REASONABLE WATCHFULNESS SHOULD BE SUFFICIENT TO AVOID SNAKEBITE.

In U.S. states such as Arizona, New Mexico, and Texas, more people are bitten by the western diamondback than by any other type of rattlesnake.

Fact or Fiction?

The western diamondback will starve to death if it loses one of its fangs.

FICTION! The rattlesnake has replacement fangs growing at all times to fill any gap—and keep that bite just right.

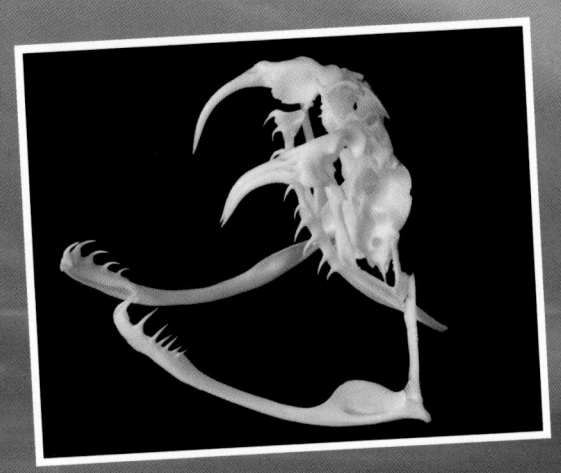

Rattlesnakes don't always inject venom when they bite. These attacks are called "dry bites."

Sure, the western diamondback may be as tough as old boots. But it's also kind of shy and doesn't go sneaking around looking for trouble. That doesn't stop people from looking for the diamondback.

Thousands of the reptiles are harvested every year in rattlesnake roundups. Organizers say the events control the snake **population** and keep people and farm animals safe.

The annual Morris Rattlesnake Roundup in Pennsylvania includes a snake hunting competition, music performances, and fireworks.

And there are lots of rattlesnakes! Nearly 25,000 pounds (11,340 kilograms) of snakes were bagged in one roundup in the small town of Sweetwater, Texas.

That's about as heavy as a school bus full of kids!

The rounded-up rattlesnakes are sold so their skin can be used to make leather bags, belts, and cowboy boots.

Rattlesnake Roundup in Sweetwater, Texas

A Bellyful of Belly Crawlers!

Captured diamondbacks can also end up on a cookout menu. Doesn't a nice warm bowl of rattlesnake chili or a plate of cowboy snake cakes sound delicioussssss?

Glossary

cunning (KUHN-ing): clever at tricking

distinctive (diss-TINGK-tiv): different from all others

hibernate (HYE-bur-nate): spend winter in a deep sleep

litter (LIT-ur): group of animals born at the same time to one mother

nocturnal (nok-TUR-nuhl): to do with the night, or happening at night

population (pop-yuh-LAY-shuhn): total number of people who live in a place

protein (PROH-teen): substance found in all living plant and animal cells

puny (PYOO-nee): small and weak, or unimportant

species (SPEE-sheez): one of the groups into which animals and plants of the same genus are divided according to their shared characteristics

venom (VEN-uhm): poison produced by some snakes and spiders; usually passed into a victim's body through a bite or sting

Index

America(s) 4, 15, 23
baby(ies) 20
burrow 10
eggs 20
fangs 14, 21, 25
humans 11
hunter(s) 6, 8
mating 20
prey 9, 13, 14, 15, 16
rattle 16, 18, 19, 21
reptile(s) 10, 27
shed 21
skin 18, 21, 28
tail 4, 16, 19
viper 13

Show What You Know

1. What are some of the animals eaten by the western diamondback rattlesnake?

2. Why is a cave or burrow important to a western diamondback rattlesnake?

3. How do rattlesnakes help stop people from getting diseases?

4. Rattlesnake meat is used to make chili and other dishes. What are some unusual foods you have eaten?

5. When does a western diamondback get a new rattle?

Further Reading

Bowman, Chris, *Western Diamondback Rattlesnakes*, Epic, 2014.

Discovery Channel, *Discovery Snakeopedia: The Complete Guide to Everything Snakes - Plus Lizards and More Reptiles*, Liberty Street, 2014.

Gagne, Tammy, *Snakes: Built for the Hunt*, Capstone Press, 2016.

About the Author

Gary Sprott is a writer in Tampa, Florida. He loves reading, watching soccer, and spending time at the beach with his family. He's not too scared of snakes—so long as they stay on the pages of a book!

Meet The Author!
www.meetREMauthors.com

© 2019 Rourke Educational Media

All rights reserved. No part of this book may be reproduced or utilized in any form or by any means, electronic or mechanical including photocopying, recording, or by any information storage and retrieval system without permission in writing from the publisher.

www.rourkeeducationalmedia.com

PHOTO CREDITS: Cover & Title Pg ©PhilBilly, Pg 4 ©By Ryan M. Bolton, Pg 6 ©DamianKuzdak, ©Zenya Aksonenko, Pg 7 ©simazoran, ©Bartfett, Pg 8 ©Loretta Hostettler, Pg 11 ©Bill Gorum/Alamy Stock Photo, ©shaunl, Pg 12 ©By fivespots, Pg 14 ©Mikaelmales|Dreamstime.com, Pg 17 ©Danita Delimont/Alamy Stock Photo, Pg 18 ©F1online digitale Bildagentur GmbH/Alamy Stock Photo, Pg 19 ©MediaProduction, ©Mark Kostich, Pg 20 ©By Steve Shoup, Pg 21 ©Sylvia Schug, Pg 22 ©ian600f, Pg 23 ©Bill Gorum/Alamy Stock Photo, ©JasonOndreicka, Pg 24 ©By Aaron Kohr, Pg 25 ©DCorn, ©Mark Kostich, Pg 26 ©ViktorLoki, Pg 27 ©Splash News/Alamy Stock Photo, Pg 29 ©Richard Ellis/Alamy Stock Photo, ©FotoShoot

Edited by: Keli Sipperley
Cover by: Kathy Walsh
Interior design by: Corey Mills and Rhea Magaro-Wallace

Library of Congress PCN Data

Western Diamondback Rattlesnake / Gary Sprott
(World's Coolest Snakes)
ISBN 978-1-64156-485-4 (hard cover)
ISBN 978-1-64156-611-7 (soft cover)
ISBN 978-1-64156-724-4 (e-Book)
Library of Congress Control Number: 2018930704

Rourke Educational Media
Printed in the United States of America,
North Mankato, Minnesota

597.963 S   CEN
Sprott, Gary,
   Western diamondback rattlesnake /

CENTRAL LIBRARY
03/19